MW01156221

File-Folder Games in COLOR
Science

by Immacula A. Rhodes

New York • Toronto • London • Auckland • Sydney
Mexico City • New Delhi • Hong Kong • Buenos Aires

Teaching Resources

To Jimmy,
My cousin, my brother, my friend

"Whatever is true, whatever is noble, whatever is right, whatever is pure, whatever is lovely, whatever is admirable—if anything is excellent or praiseworthy—think about such things."

— Philippians 4:8

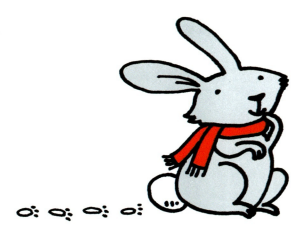

Cover design by Jason Robinson
Interior design by Solas
Cover and interior illustrations by Rusty Fletcher

ISBN-13: 978-0-439-51764-5
ISBN-10: 0-439-51764-8

1 2 3 4 5 6 7 8 9 10   40   16 15 14 13 12 11 10 09

Contents

File-Folder Games

About This Book

File-Folder Games in Color: Science offers an engaging and fun way to motivate children of all learning styles and help them build vocabulary and essential reading skills while reinforcing science-related concepts. Research shows that repetition and multiple exposure to content-area words and concepts enhance vocabulary development and comprehension. The games in this book are also designed to help children meet important curriculum standards. (See Meeting the Science and Language Arts Standards, page 6, for more.)

The games are a snap to set up and store: Just tear out the full-color game boards from this book, glue them inside file folders, and you've got ten instant learning center activities. Children will have fun as they learn about animal babies and parents in Nature's Nursery, move raindrops through the water cycle in Raindrops Go Round, explore life cycles in Caterpillar Chat, discover interesting facts in Space Adventures, and much more.

What's Inside

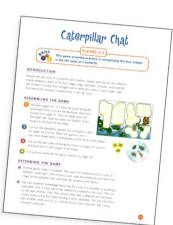

Each game includes the following:

- an introductory page for the teacher that provides a suggestion for introducing the game

- step-by-step assembly directions

- Extending the Game activities to continue reinforcing children's skills and interest

- a label with the title of each game for the file-folder tab

- a pocket to attach to the front of the file folder for storing the game parts

- directions that explain to children how to play the game

- an answer key

- game cards

- one or more game boards

- some games also include game markers and a game cube, number pyramid, or spinner

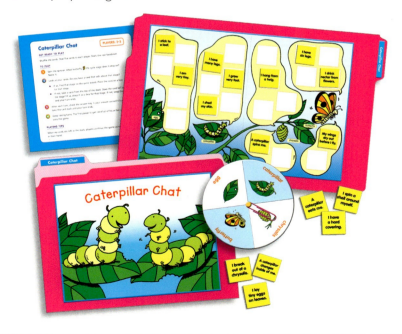

Making the File-Folder Games

In addition to the game pages, you will need the following:

- 10 file folders (in a variety of colors, if possible)
- scissors
- clear packing tape
- glue stick or rubber cement
- paper clips
- brass fasteners

Tips

- Back the spinners, game cubes, number pyramids, and game markers with tagboard before assembling. Laminate for durability.

- Before cutting apart the game cards, make additional copies (in color or black and white) for use with the Extending the Game activities.

- Place the accessories for each game, such as spinners, game cubes, number pyramids, and game markers in separate, labeled zipper storage bags. Keep the bags in a basket near the games.

Using the File-Folder Games

- Before introducing the games to children, conduct mini-lessons to review the science vocabulary and concept used in each game.

- Model how to play each game. You might also play it with children the first time.

- Give children suggestions on how to determine the order in which players take turns, such as rolling a die and taking turns in numerical order.

- Store the games in a learning center and encourage children to play in pairs or small groups before or after school, during free choice time, or when they have finished other tasks.

- Send the games home for children to play with family members and friends.

- Use the Extending the Game activities to continue reinforcing children's skills and interest.

Storage Ideas

Keep the file-folder games in any of these places:

- science center
- vertical file tray
- file box
- file cabinet
- bookshelf
- plastic stacking crate

What the Research Says

In an effective early science curriculum vocabulary development is essential to building the knowledge base needed for understanding science concepts. In fact, the relationship between vocabulary and reading comprehension extends across all content areas. In its review of reading research, the National Reading Panel concluded that effective strategies for building children's vocabulary include direct and indirect instruction, repeated meaningful exposure to new words, and rich and varied contexts for learning. Children learn content-area vocabulary best from a combination of teaching methods, including purposeful interaction with the related concepts.

Meeting the Science and Language Arts Standards

Connections to the McREL Science and Language Arts Standards

Mid-continent Research for Education and Learning (McREL), a nationally recognized, nonprofit organization, has compiled and evaluated national and state standards—and proposed what teachers should provide for their students to grow proficient in language arts and science, among other curriculum areas. The games and activities in this book support the following standards:

Earth and Space Sciences
- Understands the water cycle
- Knows vocabulary for different types of weather
- Knows that water can be a liquid, a solid, or a gas and can change from one form to the other
- Understands the composition and structure of the universe and Earth's place in it
- Knows vocabulary for major features of the sky
- Knows basic patterns of the sun and moon
- Knows that the sun supplies heat and light to Earth

Life Sciences
- Knows that plants and animals closely resemble their parents
- Knows that differences exist among individuals of the same kind of plant or animal
- Knows that living things go through a process of growth and change
- Knows the basic needs of plants and animals
- Knows that plants and animals have features that help them live in different environments

- Knows that plants and animals need certain resources for energy and growth (food, water, light, air)
- Knows that distinct environments support the life of different types of plants and animals

Health
- Knows community health providers and their roles
- Knows rules for traffic and pedestrian safety
- Knows safe behaviors in the classroom and on the playground
- Knows potentially dangerous substances and objects
- Knows the routines to follow in emergency situations
- Knows basic fire, traffic, water, and recreation safety practices
- Knows that some foods are more nutritious than others
- Classifies foods and food combinations according to the food groups
- Knows basic personal hygiene habits required to maintain health

Language Arts
Uses the general skills and strategies of the reading process:
- Uses mental images based on pictures and print to aid in comprehension of text
- Uses meaning clues to aid comprehension and make predictions about content
- Understands level-appropriate sight words and vocabulary
- Uses self-correction strategies

Source: National Reading Panel. (2000). *Teaching children to read: An evidence-based assessment of the scientific research literature on reading and its implications for reading instruction: Report of the subgroups* (NIH Publication No. 00–4754). Washington, DC: National Institute of Child Health and Human Development.

Source: Kendall, J. S. & Marzano, R. J. (2004). *Content knowledge: A compendium of standards and benchmarks for K–12 education.* Aurora, CO: Mid-continent Research for Education and Learning. Online database: http://www.mcrel.org/standards-benchmarks/

Science Vocabulary and Concepts

The following lists show the science vocabulary and concepts used in each file-folder game:

Healthy and Safe!
(health and safety practices)
Ask for help.
Brush your teeth.
Call 9-1-1.
Eat healthy foods.
Exercise every day.
Get enough rest.
Look both ways.
Never play with matches.
Put on sunscreen.
Read the signs.
Stop, drop, and roll.
Take a bath.
Take turns.
Use the sidewalk.
Visit the dentist.
Visit the doctor.
Walk when indoors.
Wash your hands.
Wear a helmet.
Wear a seatbelt.

Good for Me!
(nutrition)
Milk: cheese, cottage cheese, milk, yogurt, yogurt smoothie
Meats & Beans: almonds, chicken, eggs, fish, peas, pinto beans, steak
Vegetables: broccoli, carrots, corn, peas, pinto beans, squash, sweet potatoes
Fruits: apples, bananas, grapes, oranges, pears, raisins
Grains: bread, cereal, crackers, oatmeal, pasta, rice

Super-Sleuth Senses Sack
(five senses)
almonds, blanket, book, butterfly, clock, clouds, dollar, ears, eyes, feeling, flowers, glue, grill, gum, hand, hearing, ice cream cone, lamp, lemon, moon and stars, mouse, mouth, nose, onions, pencil, perfume, picture, pillow, play dough, popcorn, radio, sight, singing, skunk, smell, snow, sound, toothpaste, touch, trumpet, wind

Nature's Nursery
(animal babies)
bear/cub, cat/kitten, cow/calf, deer/fawn, dog/puppy, duck/duckling, eagle/eaglet, elephant/calf, fish/fry, goat/kid, goose/gosling, hen/chick, horse/foal, kangaroo/joey, lion/cub, ostrich/chick, owl/owlet, pig/piglet, rabbit/kitten, seal/pup, sheep/lamb, turkey/poult, turtle/hatchling, zebra/foal

Raindrops Go Round
(water cycle)
condensation, evaporation, precipitation, rain, vapor, water

From Seed to Sunflower
(plant growth)
flower, leaves, light, roots, seed, soil, sprout, stem, water

Caterpillar Chat
(life cycle)
Egg:
I come from a butterfly.
I am very tiny.
I stick to a leaf.
I start the butterfly's life cycle.
A caterpillar grows inside of me.
A caterpillar eats me.

Caterpillar:
I eat the egg I lived in.
I have many legs.
I eat lots of leaves.
I grow very fast.
I shed my skin.
I spin a shell around myself.

Chrysalis:
A caterpillar spins me.
I hang from a twig.
I have a hard covering.
A caterpillar rests inside of me.
A caterpillar changes inside of me.
A butterfly comes out of me.

Butterfly:
I break out of a chrysalis.
My wings dry out before I fly.
I have six legs.
I use antennae to smell.
I drink nectar from flowers.
I lay tiny eggs on leaves.

Life at Lily-Pad Pond
(pond life)
beaver, bird, cattail, clam, crayfish, dragonfly, duck, eggs, fish, frog, grasshopper, lily pad, lizard, raccoon, snail, snake, tadpole, turtle, waterbug, worm

Space Adventures
(Earth, sun, and moon)
The sun is made of gas.
The sun is a star.
The sun gives us heat.
The sun gives us light.
The sun is billions of years old.
Planets orbit the sun.
A sunspot is a storm.
Earth is a planet.
Earth orbits the sun.
Earth has one moon.
Earth has living things.
Earth has water.
Earth has many kinds of weather.
Earth has many landforms.
The moon orbits Earth.
Craters are found on the moon.
Astronauts walked on the moon.
The moon has no water.
The moon is dusty.
The moon is very quiet.

It's Winter!
(animals in winter)
Animals that migrate: butterfly, goose, whale

Animals that hibernate: bat, bear, frog, groundhog, raccoon, skunk, snake, squirrel, turtle

Animals that stay active: beaver, bird, deer, fox, human, otter, rabbit, turkey

Healthy and Safe!

 SKILL

This game helps children build vocabulary and learn concepts related to health and safety practices.

INTRODUCTION

Read each game card to children and discuss the health or safety practice named on it. Ask them to tell why it is important to follow each practice. Invite children to share ways in which they engage in safe and healthy behaviors.

ASSEMBLING THE GAME

1 Remove pages 9–19 from the book along the perforated lines. Cut out the file-folder label and pocket from page 9. Glue the label onto the file-folder tab. Tape the sides and bottom of the pocket to the front of the folder.

2 Cut out the directions, answer key, and game cards on pages 11 and 13. When the game is not in use, store these items in the pocket on the front of the folder.

3 Cut out the two game boards on pages 15 and 17 and glue them to the inside of the folder.

4 Cut out and assemble the spinner on page 19.

EXTENDING THE GAME

◎ Invite children to take turns pantomiming safety or health practices. When classmates guess the activity, ask them to decide if it represents doing something the safe way or taking care of their health.

◎ Ask small groups to create posters that encourage others to practice healthy and safe behaviors. Keep the game cards nearby so children can refer to them for ideas and to check their spelling.

Healthy and Safe!

GET READY TO PLAY

- Each player chooses a game board.
- Shuffle the game cards. Stack them facedown.

TO PLAY

1 Spin the spinner. Take that number of cards. If the spinner stops on "Oops!" your turn ends.

2 Read each card. Look for a matching picture on your game board. Do you have a match?

- If so, cover the picture with the card.
- If not, put the card on the bottom of the stack.

3 Keep taking turns. The first player to cover all of his or her picture boxes wins the game.

Healthy and Safe!

ANSWER KEY

Game Board 1	Game Board 2
Take a bath.	Eat healthy foods.
Take turns.	Wear a helmet.
Use the sidewalk.	Exercise every day.
Visit the doctor.	Look both ways.
Read the signs.	Visit the dentist.
Never play with matches.	Get enough rest.
Wash your hands.	Wear a seatbelt.
Brush your teeth.	Stop, drop, and roll.
Ask for help.	Call 9-1-1.
Put on sunscreen.	Walk when indoors.

Eat healthy foods.	Wear a helmet.	Exercise every day.	Look both ways.
Visit the dentist.	Get enough rest.	Wear a seatbelt.	Stop, drop, and roll.
Call 9-1-1.	Walk when indoors.	Take a bath.	Take turns.
Use the sidewalk.	Visit the doctor.	Read the signs.	Never play with matches.
Wash your hands.	Brush your teeth.	Ask for help.	Put on sunscreen.

ENTER

KEEP
OUT

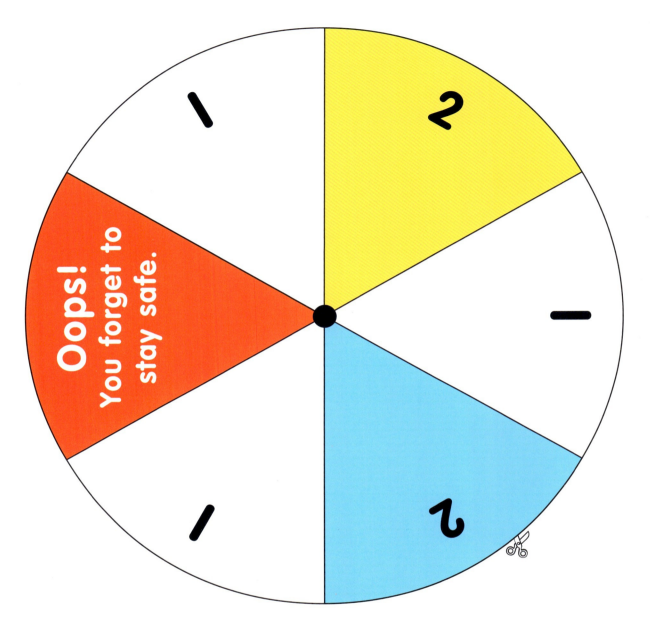

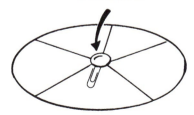

brass fastener

Assemble the spinner using a paper clip and brass fastener as shown. Make sure the paper clip spins easily.

Good for Me!

SKILL

This game provides practice in identifying the food groups on the Food Guide Pyramid and sorting foods according to the groups.

INTRODUCTION

Create a five-column chart using the food groups—excluding "oils"—as headings. Explain that the groups come from the Food Guide Pyramid, a guide that recommends which types of foods and how many of each children should eat to grow healthy and strong. Then review the game cards with children. After naming each food, have a volunteer place the card in the appropriate column on the chart. When finished, review the recommended daily servings for each food group. Also point out the importance of eating whole grains—brown rice, whole wheat bread and pasta, and so on.

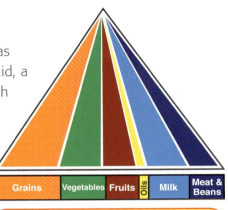

| Grains | Vegetables | Fruits | Oils | Milk | Meat & Beans |

Note: The food group "Oils" is not included in the game. When introducing the food groups, you might want to include this group in your discussion.

ASSEMBLING THE GAME

1. Remove pages 23–31 from the book along the perforated lines. Cut out the file-folder label and pocket from page 23. Glue the label onto the file-folder tab. Tape the sides and bottom of the pocket to the front of the folder.

2. Cut out the directions, answer key, and game cards on pages 25 and 27. When the game is not in use, store these items in the pocket on the front of the folder.

3. Cut out the two game boards on pages 29 and 31 and glue them to the inside of the folder.

EXTENDING THE GAME

Have children write a different food group and the recommended daily servings on one of six paper plates. Then ask them to draw or glue on pictures of their favorite foods in each group. When finished, have them stack and staple the plates to a paper-plate cover titled "Good for Me!"

Good for Me!

GET READY TO PLAY

- Each player chooses a game board.
- Shuffle the cards. Deal three cards to each player. Stack the rest facedown.

TO PLAY

1 Check your cards. Do you have a food that belongs to a food group on your game board?

- If so, name the food. Place the card on a matching box. Then take a card from the top of the stack.
- If not, put the card on the bottom of the stack. Take the top card. Then your turn ends.

2 After each turn, check the answer key. Is your answer correct? If not, take the card back.

3 Keep taking turns. The first player to cover all of his or her food group boxes calls out "Good for Me!" That player wins the game.

PLAYING TIPS

- Players may play only one card on each turn.
- If no cards are left in the stack, players trade one of their cards with each other.
- Pinto beans and peas fit into both the Meats & Beans and Vegetables groups.

Good for Me!

ANSWER KEY

Milk: cheese, cottage cheese, milk, yogurt, yogurt smoothie

Meats & Beans: almonds, chicken, eggs, fish, peas, pinto beans, steak

Vegetables: broccoli, carrots, corn, peas, pinto beans, squash, sweet potatoes

Fruits: apples, bananas, grapes, oranges, pears, raisins

Grains: bread, cereal, crackers, oatmeal, pasta, rice

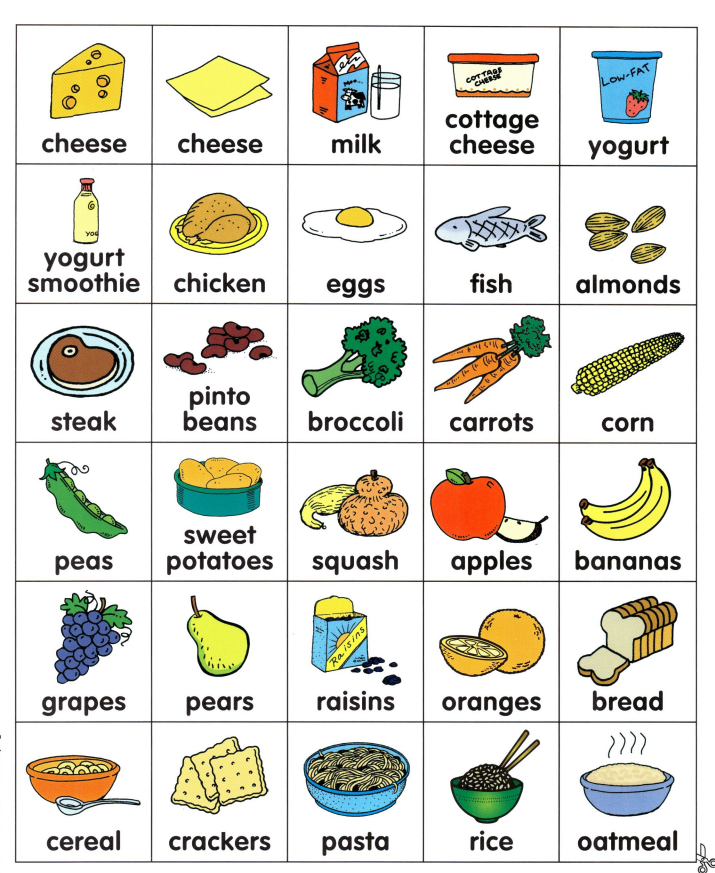

cheese	cheese	milk	cottage cheese	yogurt
yogurt smoothie	chicken	eggs	fish	almonds
steak	pinto beans	broccoli	carrots	corn
peas	sweet potatoes	squash	apples	bananas
grapes	pears	raisins	oranges	bread
cereal	crackers	pasta	rice	oatmeal

Glue this page to the left side of the file folder.

Fruit Group
Fruit Group
Fruit Group
Vegetable Group
Vegetable Group
Vegetable Group
Grains Group
Grains Group
Meats & Beans Group
Meats & Beans Group
Milk Group
Milk Group

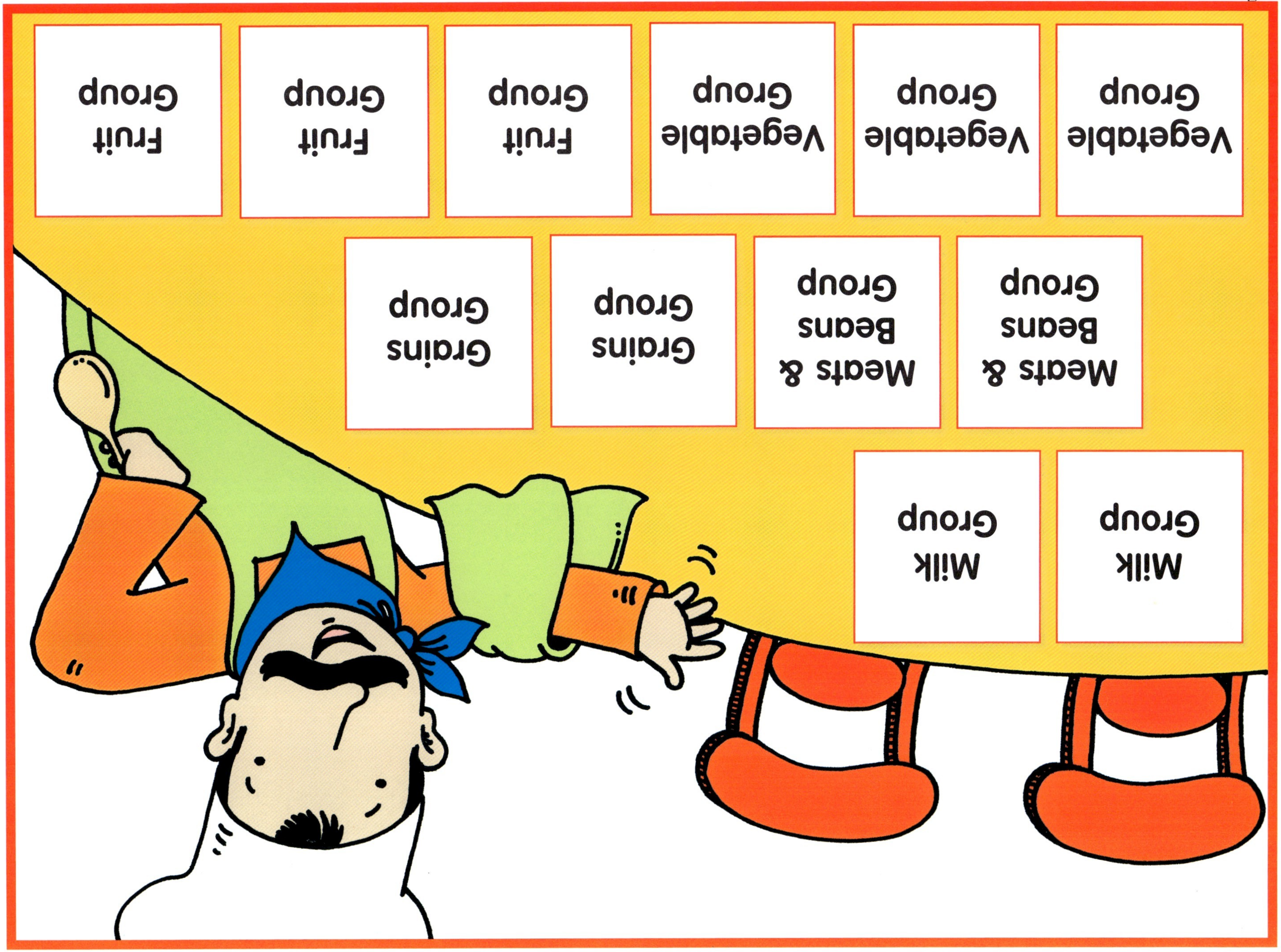

Super-Sleuth Senses Sack

 SKILL

This game provides practice in identifying how the five senses are used to learn about things in our world.

INTRODUCTION

Write the names for the five senses on the board. Then review the picture cards with children. Ask them to tell which senses they might use to identify the object or concept represented by each picture. Can they use more than one of the senses? Invite them to explain their answers. Then show and explain the symbols from the game that are used to represent the five senses: an eye, ear, hand, nose, and mouth.

ASSEMBLING THE GAME

1 Remove pages 35–45 from the book along the perforated lines. Cut out the file-folder label and pocket from page 35. Glue the label onto the file-folder tab. Tape the sides and bottom of the pocket to the front of the folder.

2 Cut out the directions, answer key, and game cards on pages 37 and 39. When the game is not in use, store these items in the pocket on the front of the folder.

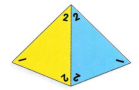

3 Cut out the two game boards on pages 41 and 43 and glue them to the inside of the folder.

4 Cut out and assemble the number pyramid on page 45.

EXTENDING THE GAME

◎ Give each child a picture card. Then call out one of the five senses. Ask children to stand if they can use the named sense to learn about the picture on their card. Invite each child to explain his or her response.

◎ Have children write about and illustrate their favorite thing to see, hear, smell, taste, and touch, creating a separate page for each of the five senses. Next, have them assemble their pages into a booklet titled "My Favorite Sensations."

Super-Sleuth Senses Sack

GET READY TO PLAY

- Each player chooses a game board.
- Shuffle the cards. Stack them facedown.

TO PLAY

1 Roll the number pyramid. Take that number of cards.

2 Name the picture on each card. Does it go with a sense on your game board?

  - If so, tell how the sense is used with each picture. Then place each card on its matching sense box.
  - If not, put the card on the bottom of the stack.

3 After each turn, check the answer key. Is each answer correct? If not, put that card on the bottom of the stack.

4 Keep taking turns. The first player to cover all of his or her sense boxes calls out "Super Sleuth!" That player wins the game.

Super-Sleuth Senses Sack

ANSWER KEY

Sight: almonds, blanket, book, butterfly, clock, clouds, dollar, flowers, glue, grill, gum, ice cream cone, lamp, lemon, moon and stars, mouse, onions, pencil, perfume, picture, pillow, play dough, popcorn, radio, skunk, snow, toothpaste, trumpet

Hearing: clock, mouse, pencil, popcorn, radio, singing, trumpet, wind

Touch/Feeling: almonds, blanket, book, butterfly, clock, dollar, flowers, glue, grill, gum, ice cream cone, lamp, lemon, mouse, onions, pencil, perfume, picture, pillow, play dough, popcorn, radio, skunk, snow, toothpaste, trumpet, wind

Smell: almonds, book, dollar, flowers, glue, grill, gum, ice cream cone, lemon, onions, perfume, play dough, popcorn, skunk, toothpaste

Taste: almonds, gum, ice cream cone, lemon, onions, popcorn, toothpaste

(Other answers may be accepted if players can explain their reasoning.)

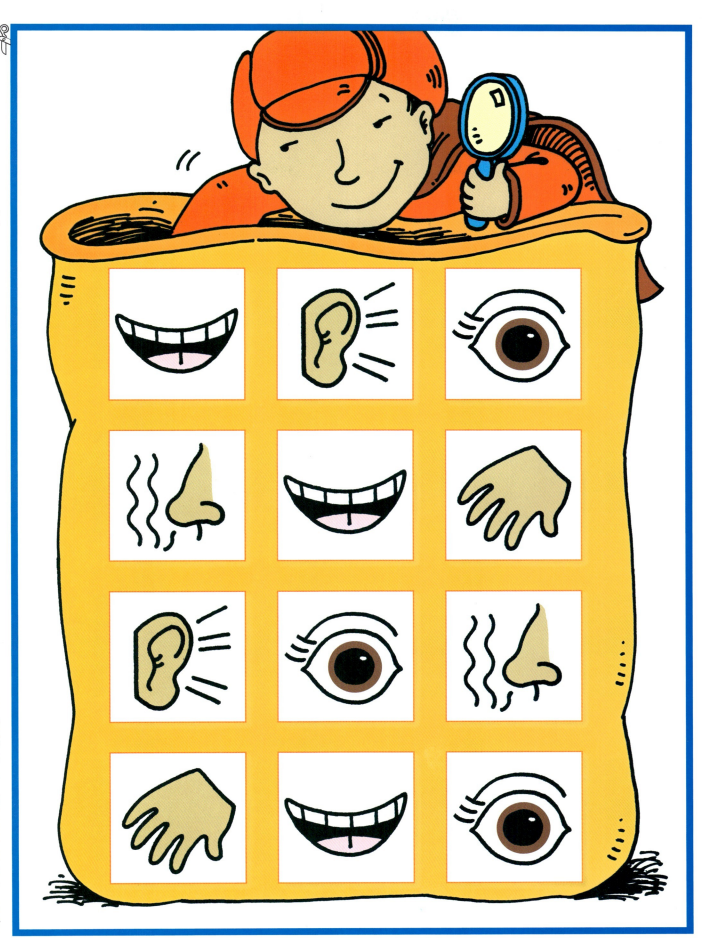

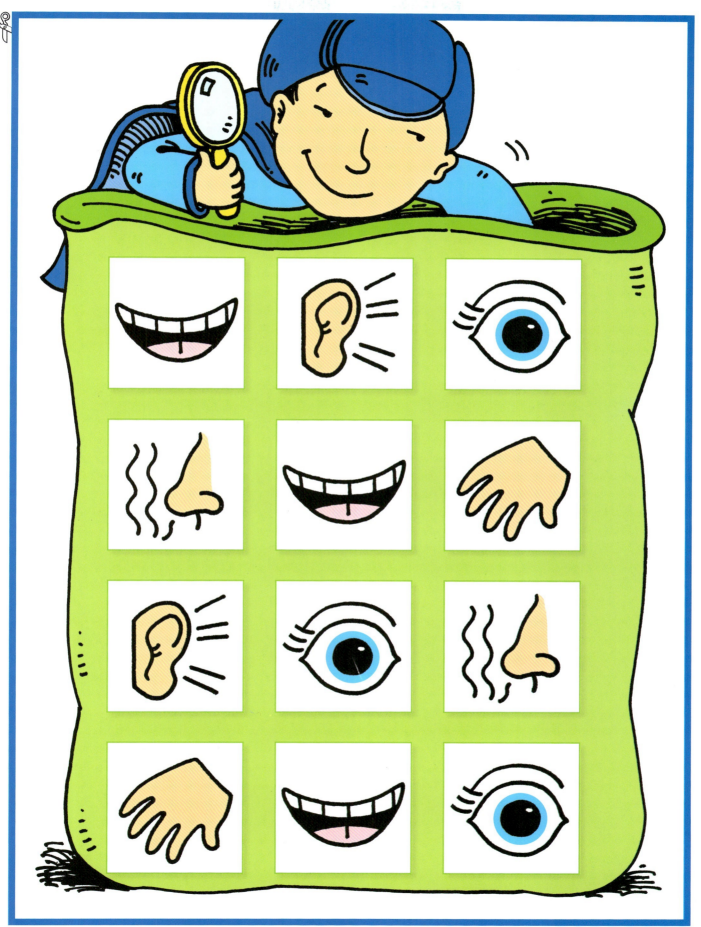

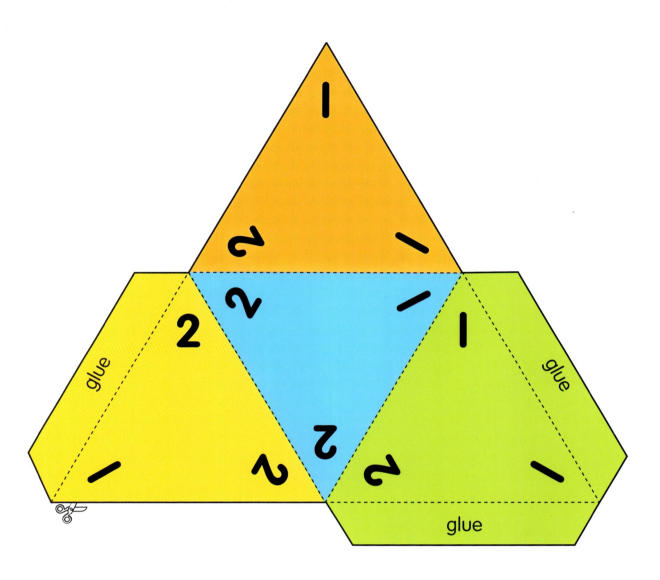

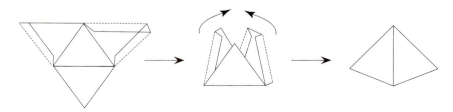

Assemble the pyramid by folding as shown. Glue closed.

Nature's Nursery

INTRODUCTION

Explain to students that young animals often have a different name than their parents. Write a parent animal name from the game (such as *cow*) on chart paper. Ask children to give the name for its baby (*calf*). Then, one at a time, add the other parent animals and babies to the list, discussing the names for each. Point out that the same name is sometimes given to different animal babies. For example, a *kitten* refers to a baby cat and a baby rabbit.

ASSEMBLING THE GAME

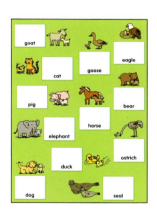

1. Remove pages 49–59 from the book along the perforated lines. Cut out the file-folder label and pocket from page 49. Glue the label onto the file-folder tab. Tape the sides and bottom of the pocket to the front of the folder.

2. Cut out the directions, answer key, and game cards on pages 51 and 53. When the game is not in use, store these items in the pocket on the front of the folder.

3. Cut out the two game boards on pages 55 and 57 and glue them to the inside of the folder.

4. Cut out and assemble the number pyramid on page 59.

EXTENDING THE GAME

◎ Play animal charades using the animal names from the game. Let children guess the mystery animal and also provide the name of its baby.

◎ Invite children to create parent and animal baby puppets. Have two or more students collaborate to write a short script for their puppets. Then have them use their puppets to act out the mini-play for the class.

Nature's Nursery

Nature's Nursery

GET READY TO PLAY

- Each player chooses a game board.
- Shuffle the cards. Stack them facedown.

TO PLAY

1 Roll the number pyramid. Take that number of cards.

2 Read the baby animal name on each card. Does it belong with a parent name on your game board?
- If so, place that card on its matching box.
- If not, put the card on the bottom of the stack.

3 After each turn, check the answer key. Is each answer correct? If not, put that card on the bottom of the stack.

4 Keep taking turns. The first player to cover all of his or her parent animal boxes wins the game.

Nature's Nursery

ANSWER KEY

Game Board 1 (left side)

Parent	Baby
goat	kid
goose	gosling
eagle	eaglet
cat	kitten
pig	piglet
horse	foal
bear	cub
elephant	calf
ostrich	chick
dog	puppy
duck	duckling
seal	pup

Game Board 2 (right side)

Parent	Baby
sheep	lamb
kangaroo	joey
rabbit	kitten
lion	cub
hen	chick
zebra	foal
cow	calf
owl	owlet
turkey	poult
turtle	hatchling
fish	fry
deer	fawn

calf	piglet	kid	duckling
foal	chick	puppy	kitten
kitten	lamb	poult	joey
fawn	foal	cub	cub
owlet	eaglet	gosling	calf
chick	fry	hatchling	pup

goat

eagle

cat

goose

pig

bear

elephant

horse

duck

ostrich

dog

seal

sheep

kangaroo

lion

rabbit

hen

cow

zebra

owl

turtle

fish

turkey

deer

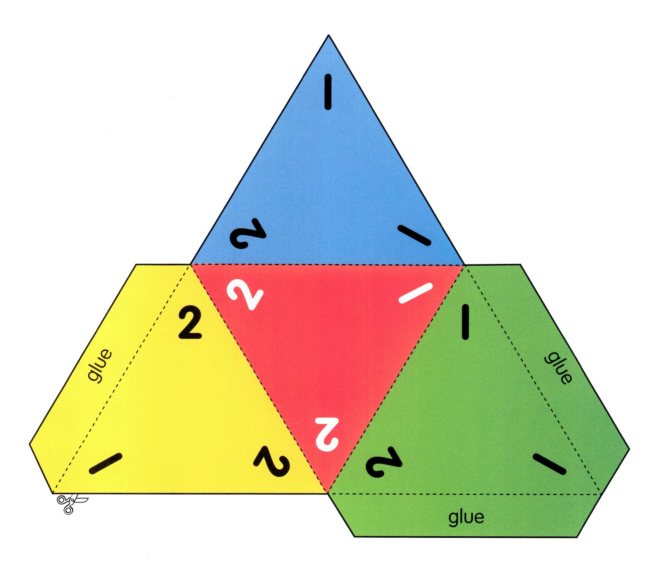

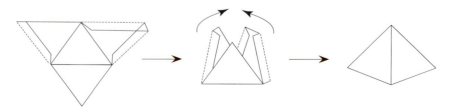

Assemble the pyramid by folding as shown. Glue closed.

Raindrops Go Round

SKILL

This game provides practice in recognizing the different processes of the water cycle and how they work together.

INTRODUCTION

Review with students the three processes of the water cycle: evaporation, condensation, and precipitation. (See Fact Finder on page 65.) Explain that the water cycle is nature's way of recycling rain. Then describe how the three processes work together to recycle rain (or the different forms of rain: snow, sleet, and hail).

ASSEMBLING THE GAME

1 Remove pages 63–73 from the book along the perforated lines. Cut out the file-folder label and pocket from page 63. Glue the label onto the file-folder tab. Tape the sides and bottom of the pocket to the front of the folder.

2 Cut out the directions, Fact Finder, and game markers on pages 65 and 67. Store each set of ten game markers in a separate zipper storage bag. When the game is not in use, store these items in the pocket on the front of the folder.

3 Cut out the two sides of the game board on pages 69 and 71 and glue them to the inside of the folder.

4 Cut out and assemble the game cube on page 73.

Game Tips
- For a shorter game, have each player use fewer markers.
- To continue the water cycle, players move their markers to Start and play again.

EXTENDING THE GAME

To let children express ways that the water cycle impacts the world, ask them to hold hands in a circle. Have the first child repeat and complete the sentence, "I know the water cycle works because _____." Then the child gently squeezes the next child's hand to signal his or her turn. Challenge children to give as many different responses as possible, such as "rain waters the plants," and "I have water to drink."

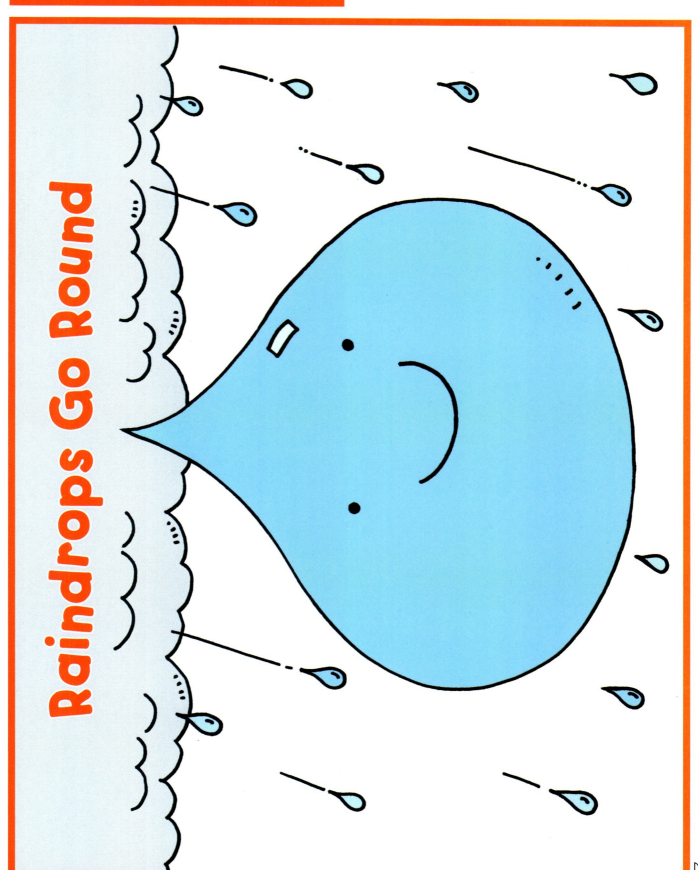

Raindrops Go Round

Raindrops Go Round

GET READY TO PLAY

- Each player chooses a set of raindrop game markers.
- Players stack their markers on the matching START box.

TO PLAY

1 Roll the game cube. Move one marker that number of spaces. Follow any directions on the space.

2 On each turn, move one marker at a time.
Move it along the Evaporation path toward a matching box in the cloud.

(You must move all ten markers from START to the cloud before moving any out of the cloud.)

3 Move one marker at a time out of the cloud.
Move it along the Condensation and Precipitation paths toward the matching FINISH box.

4 Keep taking turns. The first player to move all of his or her markers onto the FINISH box wins the game.

PLAYING TIP

Players may land on and share the same space.

Raindrops Go Round

FACT FINDER

HOW THE WATER CYCLE WORKS

1. Evaporation
- The sun heats up water on the ground.
- The water turns into tiny drops of vapor.
- The water vapor rises into the sky.

2. Condensation
- A cloud forms from the water vapor.
- Water drops begin to form in the cloud.
- The water drops grow bigger.

3. Precipitation
- The water drops fall from the cloud to make rain.
- In the winter, snow or sleet falls from the clouds.
- Water on the ground evaporates and the cycle starts again.

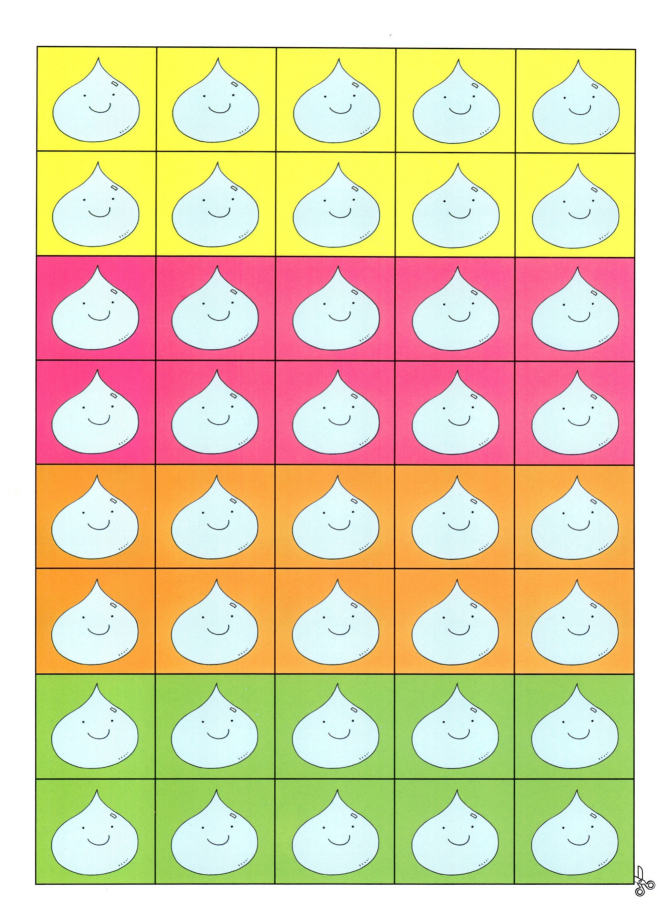

Rain evaporates slowly. Go back 1.

Rain evaporates fast. Go to cloud.

Eva

Water vapor condenses too slowly. Go back to cloud.

Cloud gets heavy. Go ahead 1.

Condensation

Form a water drop. Go ahead 1.

Drop is too tiny to fall. Go back to cloud.

Fall into ocean. Go to FINISH.

uo

Cut along this edge and attach to page 71.

Cut along this edge and attach to page 69

Fall on hot roof. Go back to cloud.
Fall on plant. Go ahead 1.
Precipitati
poration
Rain is too heavy. Go back to START.
FINISH
FINISH
FINISH
FINISH
START
START
START
START

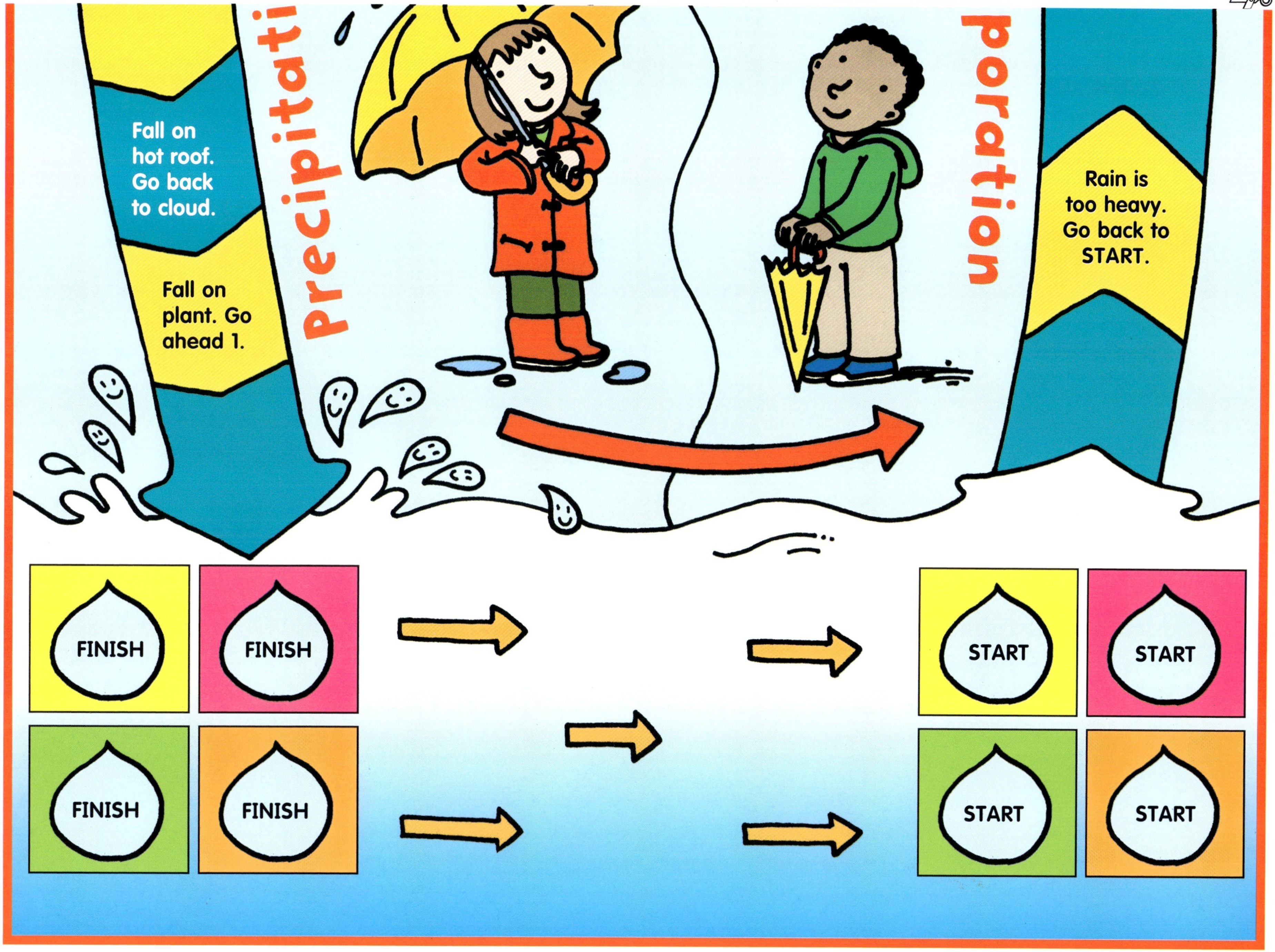

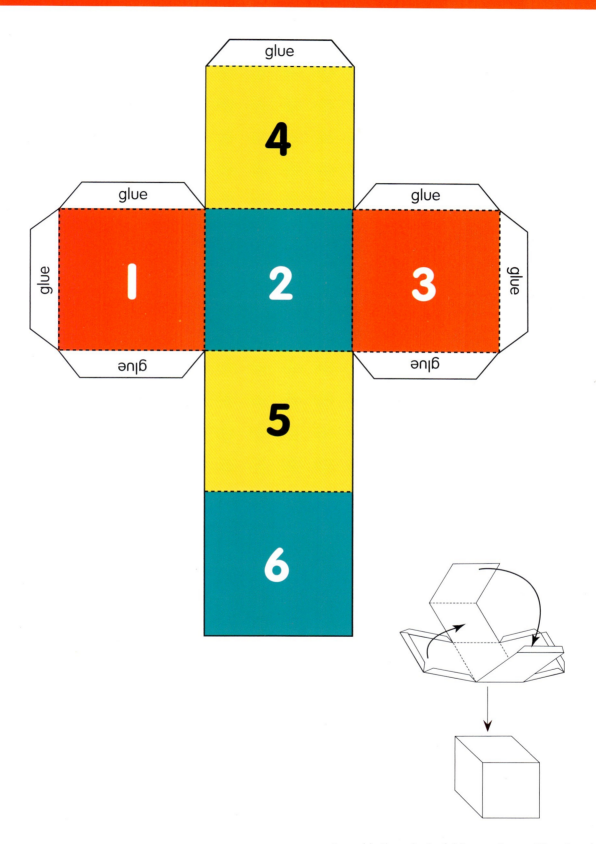

glue

4

glue glue glue

1 **2** **3**

glue glue

5

6

Assemble the cube by folding as shown. Glue closed.

From Seed to Sunflower

SKILL

This game provides practice in recognizing different parts of a plant and its growth process.

INTRODUCTION

Discuss with children the growth process of a plant from seed to bloom, including the needs of a plant and its different parts. As you demonstrate, show students the game cards in sequence for plant stages 1, 2, 3, and 4. Also, use the names of the different stages of plant growth from a gameboard. Finally, invite volunteers to place each game card on the appropriate square to show the growth stages of a plant and its different parts.

ASSEMBLING THE GAME

1. Remove pages 77–87 from the book along the perforated lines. Cut out the file-folder label and pocket from page 77. Glue the label onto the file-folder tab. Tape the sides and bottom of the pocket to the front of the folder.

2. Cut out the directions, answer key, and game cards on pages 79 and 81. Place each set of 13 game cards in a separate zipper storage bag. When the game is not in use, store these items in the pocket on the front of the folder.

3. Cut out the two game boards on pages 83 and 85 and glue them to the inside of the folder.

4. Cut out and assemble the number pyramid on page 87.

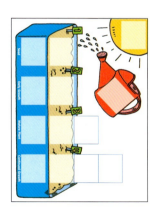
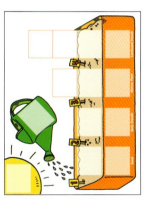

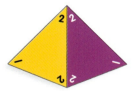

EXTENDING THE GAME

While playing a selection of soft music, narrate a dramatized version of the growth of a plant, from seed to bloom. Include emotions the plant might have and things it might see and experience during its growth. Invite children to take the role of the plant and act out the story as it unfolds.

From Seed to Sunflower

From Seed to Sunflower

GET READY TO PLAY

- Each player chooses a game board and a set of game cards.
- Players spread their cards face up.

TO PLAY

1 Roll the number pyramid. Take that number of cards for Stage 1.

2 Place each card on its matching box for Stage 1.
Do you have enough cards to cover all of the Stage 1 boxes?
If not, take cards for Stage 1 on your next turn.

3 After each turn, check the answer key. Is each answer correct?
If not, take that card back.

4 Keep taking turns. Cover the boxes for each stage in order.
The first player to cover all of his or her boxes wins the game.

PLAYING TIPS

- Players must complete each stage in order.
- The light ☀ and water ▦ cards can be played at any time.

From Seed to Sunflower

ANSWER KEY

On the sun: light

On the watering can: water

Stage 1, from bottom to top: soil, seed

Stage 2, from bottom to top: roots, sprout

Stage 3, from bottom to top: roots, stem, leaves

Stage 4, from bottom to top: roots, stem, leaves, flower

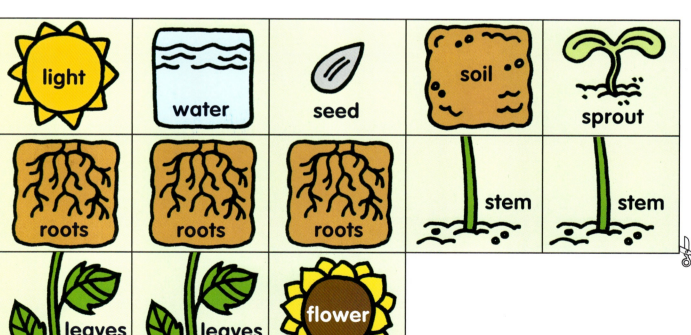

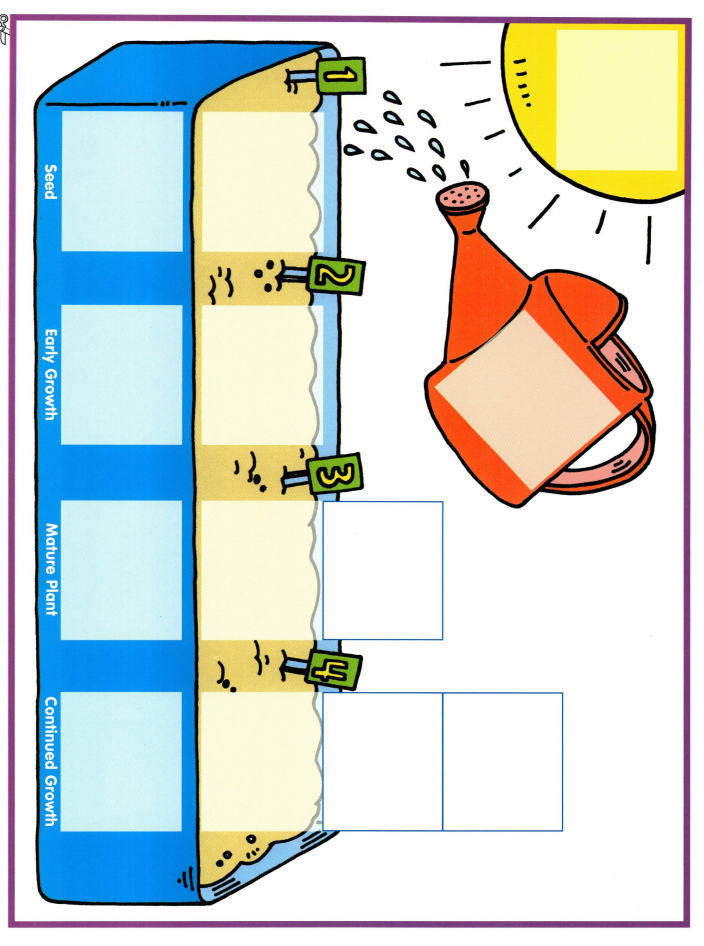

Seed

Early Growth

Mature Plant

Continued Growth

From Seed to Sunflower Game Board 1, page 85

Seed   Early Growth   Mature Plant   Continued Growth

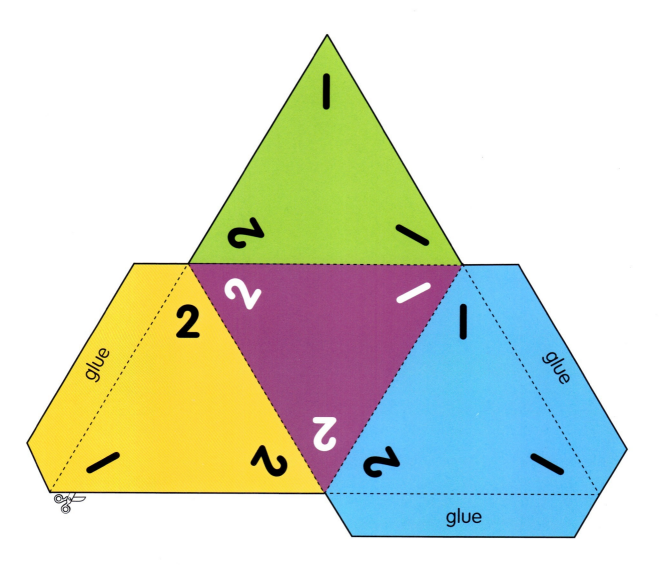

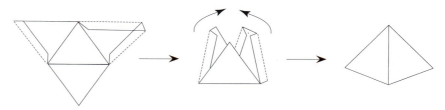

Assemble the pyramid by folding as shown. Glue closed.

Caterpillar Chat

SKILL

This game provides practice in recognizing the four stages in the life cycle of a butterfly.

INTRODUCTION

Review the life cycle of a butterfly with children. Explain and discuss the different events related to each of the four stages: egg, caterpillar, chrysalis, and butterfly. Ask children to share their thoughts about what the critter in each stage might think about the process it experiences in the life cycle.

ASSEMBLING THE GAME

1 Remove pages 91–101 from the book along the perforated lines. Cut out the file-folder label and pocket from page 91. Glue the label onto the file-folder tab. Tape the sides and bottom of the pocket to the front of the folder.

2 Cut out the directions, answer key, and game cards on pages 93 and 95. When the game is not in use, store these items in the pocket on the front of the folder.

3 Cut out the two sides of the game board on pages 97 and 99 and glue them to the inside of the folder.

4 Cut out and assemble the game spinner on page 101.

EXTENDING THE GAME

◎ Put the game cards in a basket. Then pass the basket around a circle of children. Invite each child to pick a card, read the sentence, and name the stage of the butterfly's life cycle that the sentence tells about.

◎ Tap into students' knowledge about the life cycle of a butterfly by building a caterpillar. First, a child tells a fact related to a butterfly's life cycle. Then he or she taps another child. The second child cites a different fact and then moves close to the first child, forming a short caterpillar. The first child then taps another child, and so on, until the entire class connects into a long, informed caterpillar.

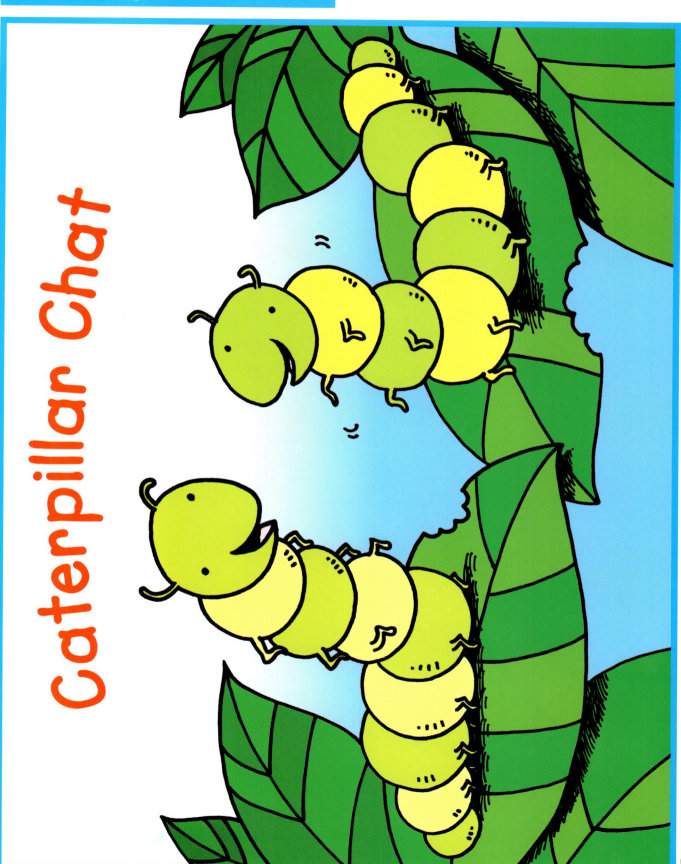

Caterpillar Chat

Caterpillar Chat

GET READY TO PLAY

Shuffle the cards. Deal five cards to each player. Stack the rest facedown.

TO PLAY

1 Spin the spinner. What butterfly  life cycle stage does it stop on? Name it.

2 Look at your cards. Do you have a card that tells about that stage?

- If so, find that stage on the game board. Place the card on a box for that stage.

- If not, take a card from the top of the stack. Does the card tell about the stage? If so, place it on a box for that stage. If not, keep the card and your turn ends.

3 After each turn, check the answer key. Is your answer correct? If not, take the card back.

4 Keep taking turns. The first player to get rid of all of his or her cards wins the game.

PLAYING TIP

When no cards are left in the stack, players continue the game using the cards in their hand.

Caterpillar Chat

ANSWER KEY

Egg:
- I come from a butterfly.
- I am very tiny.
- I stick to a leaf.
- I start the butterfly's life cycle.
- A caterpillar grows inside of me.
- A caterpillar eats me.

Caterpillar:
- I eat the egg I lived in.
- I have many legs.
- I eat lots of leaves.
- I grow very fast.
- I shed my skin.
- I spin a shell around myself.

Chrysalis:
- A caterpillar spins me.
- I hang from a twig.
- I have a hard covering.
- A caterpillar rests inside of me.
- A caterpillar changes inside of me.
- A butterfly comes out of me.

Butterfly:
- I break out of a chrysalis.
- My wings dry out before I fly.
- I have six legs.
- I use antennae to smell.
- I drink nectar from flowers.
- I lay tiny eggs on leaves.

I come from a butterfly.	I eat the egg I lived in.	A caterpillar spins me.	I break out of a chrysalis.
I am very tiny.	I have many legs.	I hang from a twig.	My wings dry out before I fly.
I stick to a leaf.	I eat lots of leaves.	I have a hard covering.	I have six legs.
I start the butterfly's life cycle.	I grow very fast.	A caterpillar rests inside of me.	I use antennae to smell.
A caterpillar grows inside of me.	I shed my skin.	A caterpillar changes inside of me.	I drink nectar from flowers.
A caterpillar eats me.	I spin a shell around myself.	A butterfly comes out of me.	I lay tiny eggs on leaves.

egg

caterpillar

butterfly

chrysalis

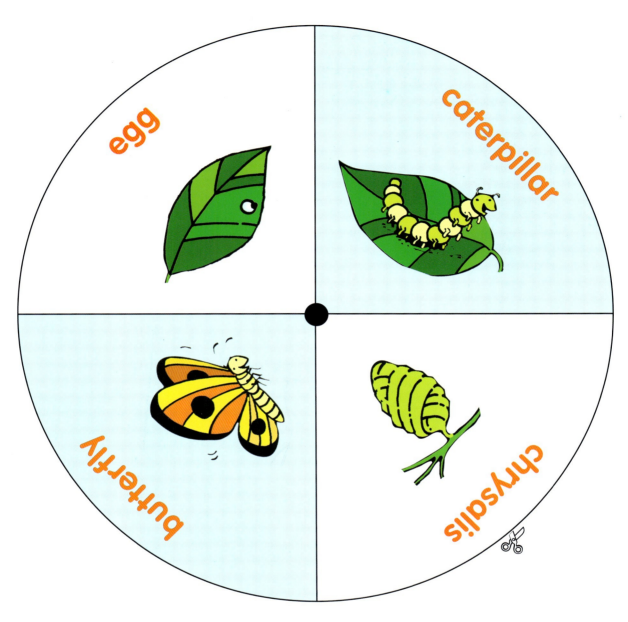

egg

caterpillar

chrysalis

butterfly

brass fastener

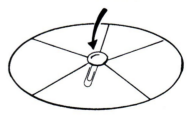

Assemble the spinner using a paper clip and brass fastener as shown. Make sure the paper clip spins easily.

Life at Lily-Pad Pond

PLAYERS: 2–3

This game provides practice in recognizing animals and other life forms in a pond environment.

INTRODUCTION

Have children brainstorm a list of animals and other types of life that can be found at a pond. Then show them each game card. If the pictured life form is already on the list, have a volunteer check that item off. If not, add it to the list. Afterward, invite children to share their personal experiences, observations, and questions about life at a pond.

ASSEMBLING THE GAME

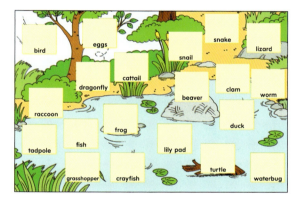

1 Remove pages 105–115 from the book along the perforated lines. Cut out the file-folder label and pocket from page 105. Glue the label onto the file-folder tab. Tape the sides and bottom of the pocket to the front of the folder.

2 Cut out the directions, answer key, game cards, and game markers on pages 107 and 109. When the game is not in use, store these items in the pocket on the front of the folder.

3 Cut out the two sides of the game board on pages 111 and 113 and glue them to the inside of the folder.

4 Cut out and assemble the number pyramid on page 115.

EXTENDING THE GAME

◎ Give small groups sheets of bulletin board paper. Have students work together to create a pond scene filled with a variety of pond life. Invite each group to tell the class about the life and activity around its pond.

◎ Ask children to take the role of frogs for this quick-thinking game. To play, name an animal, plant, or any other item that comes to mind. If the named item can be found at a pond, your little frogs leap into the air. If not, the frogs remain quiet and still.

Life at Lily-Pad Pond

Life at Lily-Pad Pond

GET READY TO PLAY

- Players place a lily-pad marker on each box on the game board.
- Shuffle the cards. Stack them facedown.

TO PLAY

1. Roll the number pyramid. Take that number of cards.

2. Name the picture on each card. Can you find its matching word on the game board?
   - If so, take the marker off the box.
     Replace it with the picture card.
   - If not, put the card on the bottom of the stack.

3. After each turn, check the answer key. Is each answer correct? If not, put that card on the bottom of the stack. Then put the marker back.

4. Keep taking turns until all of the cards are on the board.
   The player with the most markers wins.

Life at Lily-Pad Pond

ANSWER KEY

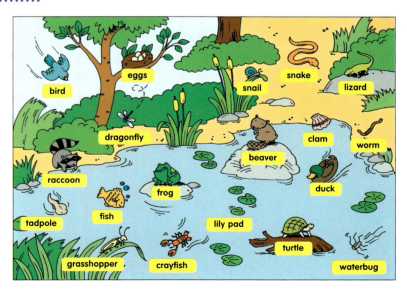

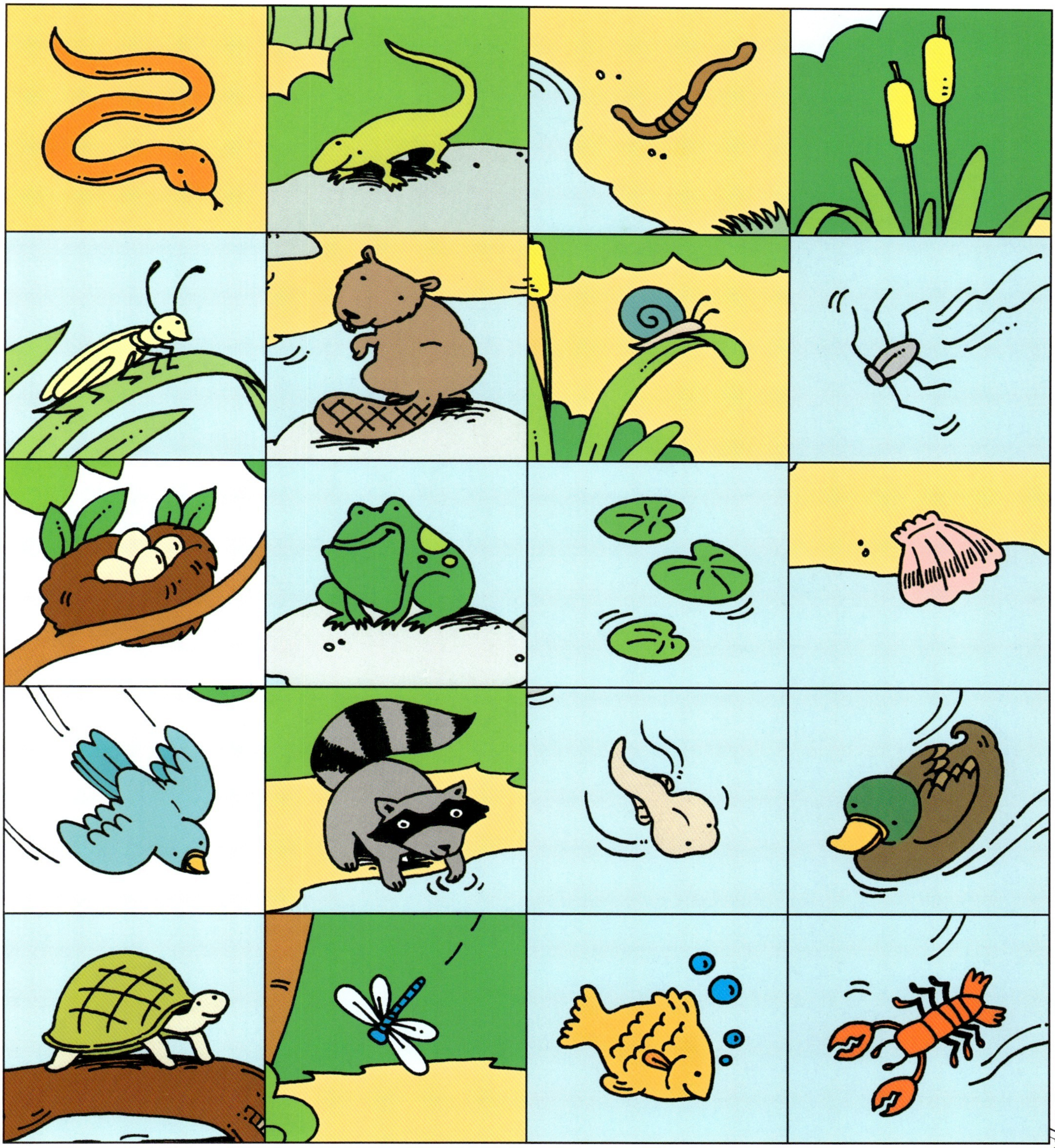

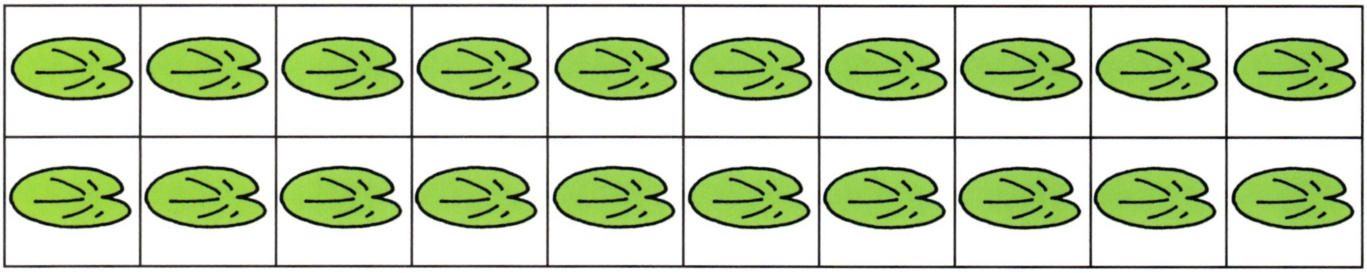

Cut along this edge and attach to page 113.

Cut along this edge and attach to page 111.

snake
lizard
snail
clam
worm
beaver
duck
lily pad
turtle
waterbug

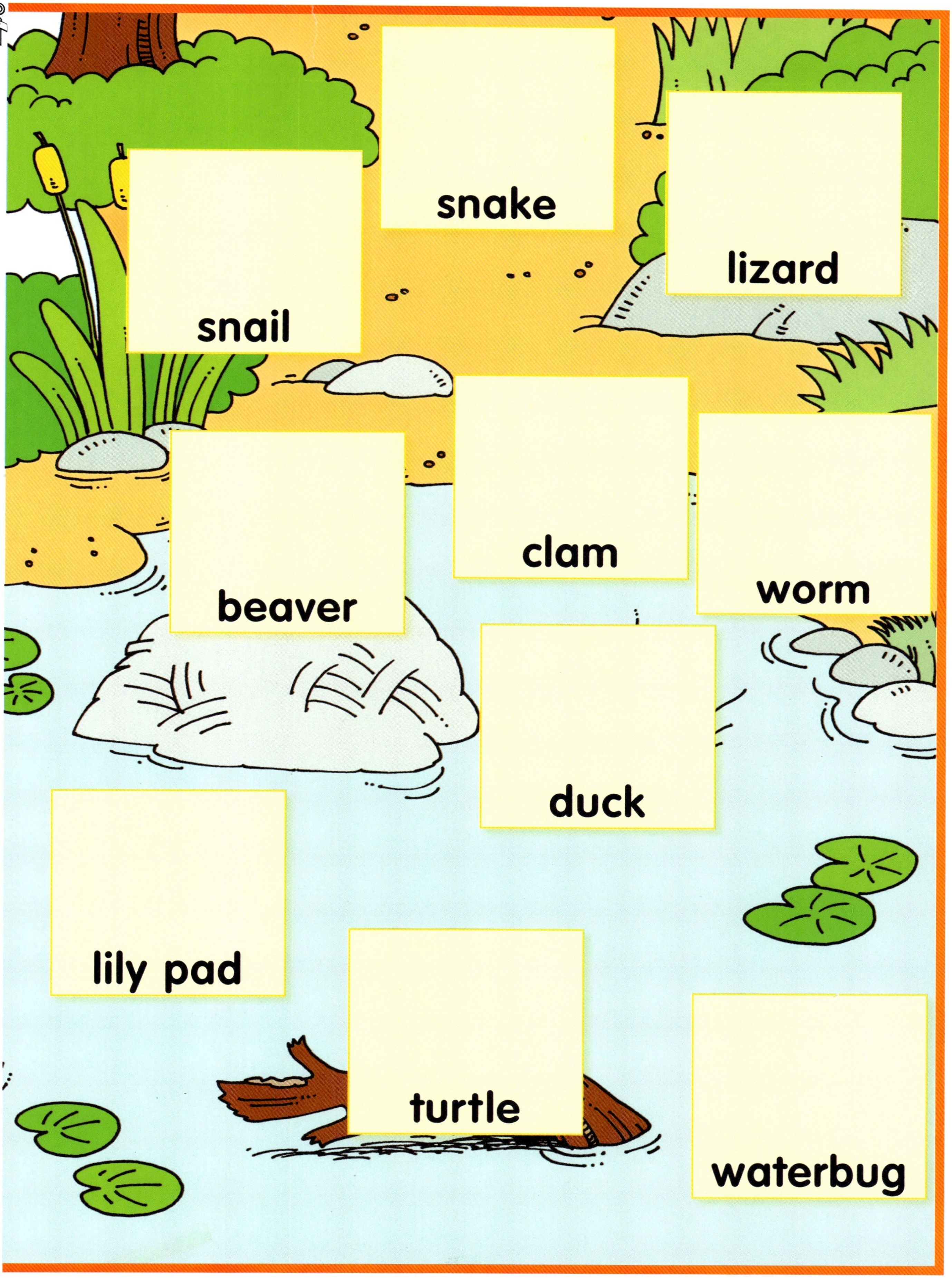

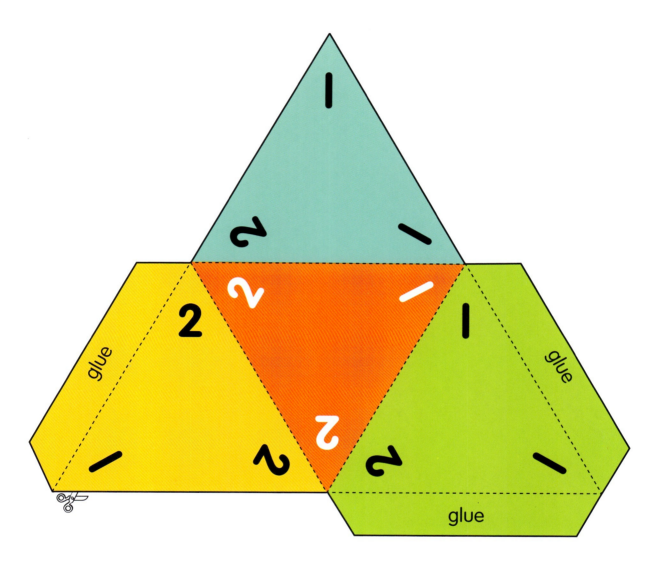

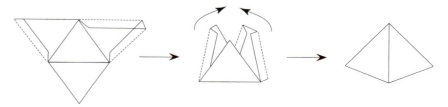

Assemble the pyramid by folding as shown. Glue closed.

Space Adventures

PLAYERS: 2-3

SKILL

This game provides practice in identifying facts about the sun, Earth, and moon.

INTRODUCTION

Create a three-column chart using "Sun," "Earth," and "Moon" as the headings. Have students brainstorm facts they know about each and write these on the chart. Then read each of the game cards and share information from the Fact Finder. (See page 121.) Have a volunteer check off the fact if it is already listed on the chart. If not, add the fact to the appropriate column.

ASSEMBLING THE GAME

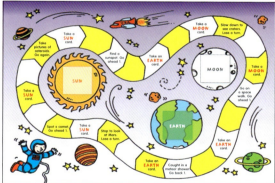

1 Remove pages 119–129 from the book along the perforated lines. Cut out the file-folder label and pocket from page 119. Glue the label onto the file-folder tab. Tape the sides and bottom of the pocket to the front of the folder.

2 Cut out the directions, Fact Finder, and game cards on pages 121 and 123. When the game is not in use, store these items in the pocket on the front of the folder.

3 Cut out the two sides of the game board on pages 125 and 127 and glue them to the inside of the folder.

4 Cut out and assemble the game cube and game markers on page 129.

EXTENDING THE GAME

◎ Invite children to draw and cut out models of the sun, Earth, and moon. Then ask them to write facts about each one on note cards. Have them use their cutouts and fact cards to create a mobile to share with classmates.

◎ Send children on an imaginary adventure into space. Tell them to make sure they bring back some interesting space specimens, such as moon dust, a shooting star, and a meteorite. When they return, invite children to share their adventures with the class and then record them in words and pictures in a booklet.

Space Adventures

GET READY TO PLAY

- Each player chooses a game marker. Place the marker on any blank space on the game board.
- Sort the fact cards into three stacks: SUN, EARTH, and MOON.
- Shuffle each stack. Place each stack on its matching box on the game board.

TO PLAY

1. Roll the game cube. Move that number of spaces. Follow any directions on the space.

2. If you take a card from one of the stacks, read it aloud. Then keep the card.

3. Keep taking turns until all of the cards have been used. The player with the most cards wins the game.

PLAYING TIPS

- Players may land on and share the same space.
- Players can move around the game board as many times as needed.

Space Adventures

FACT FINDER

ALL ABOUT ORBITS

EARTH
- Earth orbits—circles around—the sun.
- It takes Earth 365 days to orbit the sun—that's one whole year!

MOON
- The moon orbits Earth.
- It takes the moon about 30 days—or one month—to orbit Earth.

SUN
- The sun does not orbit. It is the center of our solar system.
- The Earth and other planets orbit the sun.

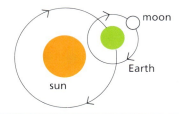

The sun is made of gas.	The sun is a star.	The sun gives us heat.	The sun gives us light.
The sun is billions of years old.	Planets orbit the sun.	A sunspot is a storm.	Earth is a planet.
Earth orbits the sun.	Earth has one moon.	Earth has living things.	Earth has water.
Earth has many kinds of weather.	Earth has many landforms.	The moon orbits Earth.	Craters are found on the moon.
Astronauts walked on the moon.	The moon has no water.	The moon is dusty.	The moon is very quiet.

SUN	SUN	SUN	SUN
EARTH	SUN	SUN	SUN
EARTH	EARTH	EARTH	EARTH
MOON	MOON	EARTH	EARTH
MOON	MOON	MOON	MOON

Take a **SUN** card.

Take pictures of asteroids. Go again.

Find a sunspot. Go ahead 1.

SUN

Take a **SUN** card.

Spot a comet. Go ahead 1.

Take a **SUN** card.

Stop to look at Mars. Lose a turn.

Cut along this edge and attach to page 127.

Take a **MOON** card.

Slow down to see craters. Lose a turn.

Take an **EARTH** card.

MOON

Take a **MOON** card.

Go on a space walk. Go ahead 1.

EARTH

Take an **EARTH** card.

Take an **EARTH** card.

Caught in a meteor shower. Go back 1.

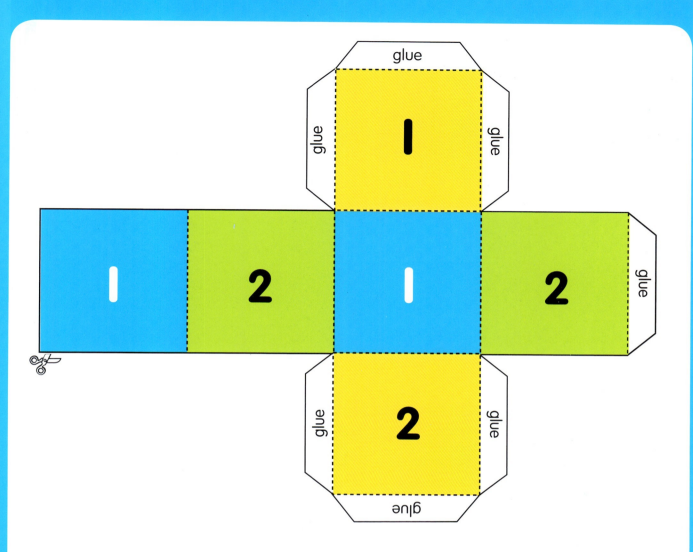

Fold the tabs on the game markers
so they stand up.

Fold here.

Fold here.

Fold here.

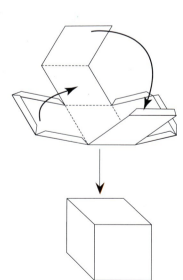

Assemble the cube by folding as shown. Glue closed.

It's Winter!

SKILL

This game provides practice in recognizing the activity of different kinds of animals in the winter.

INTRODUCTION

Create a three-column chart using "Migrate," "Hibernate," and "Stay Active" as the headings. Have students list animals that engage in each of these wintertime activities in the corresponding columns on the chart. Then read the animal name on each game card. If the animal is already on the chart, have a volunteer check off its name. If not, determine which activity the animal engages in and then add its name to the appropriate column.

ASSEMBLING THE GAME

1. Remove pages 133–143 from the book along the perforated lines. Cut out the file-folder label and pocket from page 133. Glue the label onto the file-folder tab. Tape the sides and bottom of the pocket to the front of the folder.

2. Cut out the directions, answer key, and game cards on pages 135 and 137. When the game is not in use, store these items in the pocket on the front of the folder.

3. Cut out the two sides of the game board on pages 139 and 141 and glue them to the inside of the folder.

4. Cut out and assemble the game cube and game markers on page 143.

EXTENDING THE GAME

Give each child a game card. On a signal, have children pass their cards around a circle until you call out either "Migrate," "Hibernate," or "Stay Active." At this time, children stop and read the animal names on the cards in their hands. If their animal engages in the named winter activity, they take the animal role and perform that activity. If not, they stand quietly in place until you give the next signal.

It's Winter!

It's Winter!

GET READY TO PLAY

- Each player chooses a game marker. Place the marker on any blank space on the game board.
- Shuffle the cards. Deal ten cards to each player. Spread the cards face up.

TO PLAY

1 Roll the game cube. Move that number of spaces. Name the wintertime activity on your space: Migrate, Hibernate, or Stay Active.

2 Do you have a card for an animal that does that activity? (Check the game board for clues.)

- If so, place the card on its matching activity box.
- If not, your turn ends.

3 After each turn, check the answer key. Is your answer correct? If not, take the card back.

4 Keep taking turns. The first player to get rid of all of his or her cards wins the game. (Players can move around the board as many times as needed.)

PLAYING TIP

Players may land on and share the same space.

It's Winter!

ANSWER KEY

Animals that migrate:
butterfly, goose, whale

Animals that hibernate:
bat, bear, frog, groundhog, raccoon, skunk, snake, squirrel, turtle

Animals that stay active:
beaver, bird, deer, fox, human, otter, rabbit, turkey

bat	bear	beaver	bird
butterfly	deer	frog	fox
goose	groundhog	human	otter
rabbit	raccoon	skunk	snake
squirrel	turkey	turtle	whale

Migrate

Hibernate

Cut along this edge and attach to page 141.

Stay Active

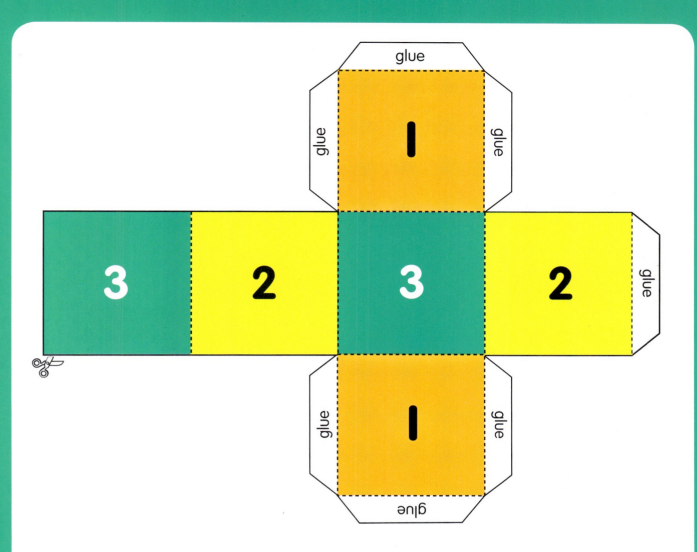

Fold the tabs on the game markers so they stand up.

Fold here.

Fold here.

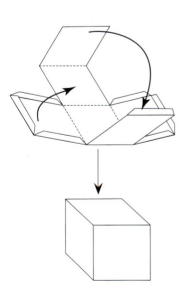

Assemble the cube by folding as shown. Glue closed.